Incredibly Easy
Skillet
recipes

Publications International, Ltd.

Pictured on the front cover: Chicken and Herb Stew *(page 18)*.
Pictured on the back cover *(top to bottom):* Quick Pasta with Peppers *(page 68)* and Asian Basil Beef and Rice *(page 115)*.

ISBN-13: 978-1-60553-711-5
ISBN-10: 1-60553-711-X

Library of Congress Control Number: 2009943160

Manufactured in China.

8 7 6 5 4 3 2 1

Microwave Cooking: Microwave ovens vary in wattage. Use the cooking times as guidelines and check for doneness before adding more time.

Preparation/Cooking Times: Preparation times are based on the approximate amount of time required to assemble the recipe before cooking, baking, chilling or serving. These times include preparation steps such as measuring, chopping and mixing. The fact that some preparations and cooking can be done simultaneously is taken into account. Preparation of optional ingredients and serving suggestions is not included.

Publications International, Ltd.

Contents

Chicken with Pomegranate-Orange Sauce (p. 16)

Chicken with Rice & Asparagus Pilaf (p. 27)

15-Minute Chicken and
Broccoli Risotto (p. 26)

Southwestern Chicken and
Black Bean Skillet (p. 17)

Chicken **Favorites**

Creamy Bow-Tie Pasta with Chicken and Broccoli

Prep Time: 10 minutes • **Cook Time:** 15 minutes

3 cups (8 ounces) farfalle (bow-tie pasta), uncooked
4 cups broccoli florets
3 tablespoons KRAFT® Roasted Red Pepper Italian with Parmesan Dressing
6 small boneless, skinless chicken breast halves (1½ pounds)
2 cloves garlic, minced
2 cups tomato-basil spaghetti sauce
4 ounces (½ of 8-ounce package) PHILADELPHIA® Neufchâtel Cheese, ⅓ Less Fat than Cream Cheese, cubed
¼ cup KRAFT® 100% Grated Parmesan Cheese

Cook pasta as directed on package, adding broccoli to the cooking water for the last 3 minutes of the pasta cooking time. Meanwhile, heat dressing in large nonstick skillet over medium heat. Add chicken and garlic; cook 5 minutes. Turn chicken over; continue cooking 4 to 5 minutes or until chicken is cooked through (170°F).

Drain pasta mixture in colander; return to pan and set aside. Add spaghetti sauce and Neufchâtel cheese to chicken in skillet; cook on medium-low heat 2 to 3 minutes or until Neufchâtel cheese is completely melted, mixture is well blended and chicken is coated with sauce, stirring occasionally. Remove chicken from skillet; keep warm. Add sauce mixture to pasta mixture; mix well. Transfer to six serving bowls.

Cut chicken crosswise into thick slices; fan out chicken over pasta mixture. Sprinkle evenly with Parmesan cheese.   *Makes 6 servings*

Greek Chicken and Artichoke Rice

2 tablespoons olive oil, divided
1 pound chicken tenders
    Paprika
¼ cup pine nuts
2 cups chicken broth
1 can (about 14 ounces) artichoke heart quarters, drained
1 cup uncooked rice
1½ tablespoons grated lemon peel
1 clove garlic
½ teaspoon salt, divided
⅛ teaspoon black pepper
    Juice of 1 lemon
2 tablespoons chopped fresh parsley
2 ounces feta cheese with sun-dried tomatoes and basil, crumbled

1. Heat 1 tablespoon oil in large skillet over medium-high heat. Sprinkle chicken lightly with paprika. Place in skillet and cook 2 minutes on one side. Remove from skillet; set aside.

2. Add pine nuts to skillet; cook 1 minute or until golden brown, stirring constantly. Add broth, artichokes, rice, lemon peel, garlic, ¼ teaspoon salt and pepper. Return chicken to skillet, seasoned side up; press down gently into rice mixture. Bring to a boil. Reduce heat; cover and simmer 15 minutes or until rice is tender.

3. Remove from heat. Drizzle with lemon juice and remaining 1 tablespoon oil. Sprinkle with remaining ¼ teaspoon salt, parsley and cheese. *Do not stir.* Serve immediately.   *Makes 4 servings*

Greek Style
Lemon Chicken

1 tablespoon olive oil
1 pound boneless skinless chicken breasts, cut into strips
2 cloves garlic, minced
2 cups MINUTE® Brown or White Rice, uncooked
1 can (14½ ounces) chicken broth
½ cup carrots, matchstick or grated
¼ cup pitted ripe olives, sliced
1 tablespoon lemon peel, grated
1 tablespoon parsley flakes
   Crumbled feta cheese (optional)
   Lemon wedges (optional)

Heat oil in large nonstick skillet over medium-high heat. Add chicken; cook and stir 6 to 8 minutes or until chicken is cooked through, adding garlic during last 3 minutes of cooking time.

Add remaining ingredients except cheese and lemon wedges; stir until well blended. Bring to a boil; cover. Remove from heat. Let stand 5 minutes. Sprinkle with feta cheese and serve with lemon wedges, if desired. *Makes 4 servings*

*Tip

Be sure to thoroughly wash cutting surfaces, utensils and your hands with hot soapy water after coming into contact with uncooked chicken. This will eliminate the risk of contaminating other foods with salmonella bacteria that is often present in raw chicken.

Chicken with Mushroom Rice Pilaf

Prep Time: 5 minutes • **Cook Time:** 30 minutes

6 to 8 chicken drumsticks (about 2.5 pounds)
1 tablespoon WESSON® Vegetable Oil
1 cup water
1 package (6.3 ounces) mushroom & herb rice pilaf mix
1 can (14.5 ounces) HUNT'S® Petite Diced Tomatoes with Mushrooms, undrained
1 cup frozen green peas

COOK chicken in oil in a large skillet over medium-high heat until browned on all sides; remove from pan.

STIR in water, rice with seasoning packet, tomatoes and peas; blend well. Top with chicken. Bring to boil; reduce heat and cover.

COOK on low for 20 to 25 minutes or until rice is tender.

Makes 4 servings

Chicken Couscous

Nonstick cooking spray
8 ounces boneless skinless chicken breast, cut into 1-inch cubes
4 zucchini, sliced
1 can (about 14 ounces) diced tomatoes
1 can (about 14 ounces) chicken broth
1 teaspoon Italian seasoning
1 cup uncooked whole wheat couscous

1. Spray large deep skillet with cooking spray; heat over medium-high heat. Cook and stir chicken 4 minutes or until lightly browned.

2. Add zucchini, tomatoes, broth and seasoning. Simmer uncovered, 15 minutes, stirring occasionally.

3. Stir in couscous; remove from heat. Cover; let stand 7 minutes. Fluff with fork before serving.

Makes 4 servings

Rosemary Chicken & Mushroom Pasta

Prep Time: 10 minutes • **Cook Time:** 20 minutes

2 tablespoons olive or vegetable oil
1½ pounds skinless, boneless chicken breasts, cut into strips
4 cups sliced mushrooms (about 12 ounces)
1 tablespoon minced garlic
1 tablespoon chopped fresh rosemary leaves *or* 1 teaspoon
dried rosemary leaves, crushed
1 can (14½ ounces) CAMPBELL'S® Chicken Gravy
1 package (1 pound) linguine or spaghetti, cooked and
drained
Shredded Parmesan cheese

1. Heat the oil in a 12-inch skillet over medium-high heat. Add the chicken and mushrooms in 2 batches and cook until the chicken is well browned, stirring often. Remove the chicken mixture from the skillet.

2. Reduce the heat to low. Stir the garlic and rosemary in the skillet and cook for 1 minute. Stir the gravy in the skillet and heat to a boil.

3. Return the chicken and mushrooms to the skillet. Cover and cook for 5 minutes or until the chicken is cooked through. Place the pasta in a large serving bowl. Pour the chicken mixture over the pasta. Toss to coat. Serve with the cheese. *Makes 6 servings*

Kitchen Tip: For a rustic twist, try whole wheat pasta in the recipe.

Chicken with Pomegranate-Orange Sauce

2 tablespoons soy sauce, divided
3 teaspoons cornstarch, divided
**1 pound boneless skinless chicken breasts, cut into
    1-inch cubes**
½ cup pomegranate juice
1 to 2 tablespoons chili garlic sauce
1 teaspoon grated orange peel
1 teaspoon grated fresh ginger
1 tablespoon vegetable or peanut oil
2 stalks celery, cut diagonally into ¼-inch slices
1 red bell pepper, cut into 1-inch-long strips
2 oranges, peeled and sectioned
3 green onions, sliced
2 cups hot cooked rice

1. Stir 1 tablespoon soy sauce into 1 teaspoon cornstarch in medium bowl until smooth. Add chicken; toss to coat. Cover; let stand 10 minutes.

2. Meanwhile, combine pomegranate juice, chili garlic sauce, remaining 1 tablespoon soy sauce, remaining 2 teaspoons cornstarch, orange peel and ginger in small bowl; stir until blended.

3. Heat oil in large nonstick skillet over medium-high heat. Add chicken; cook and stir 2 minutes. Add celery and pepper; cook and stir 3 minutes or until chicken is cooked through. Stir pomegranate juice mixture; add to skillet. Bring to a boil over high heat; reduce heat to medium and simmer 1 minute. Gently stir in orange sections; heat through. Sprinkle with green onions and serve with rice. *Makes 4 servings*

Southwestern Chicken and Black Bean Skillet

1 teaspoon ground cumin
1 teaspoon ground chili powder
½ teaspoon salt
4 boneless skinless chicken breasts
2 teaspoons canola or vegetable oil
1 cup chopped yellow onion
1 red bell pepper, chopped
1 can (about 15 ounces) black beans, rinsed and drained
½ cup chunky salsa
¼ cup chopped fresh cilantro or thinly sliced green onions (optional)

1. Combine cumin, chili powder and salt in small bowl; sprinkle evenly over both sides of chicken. Heat oil in large nonstick skillet over medium-high heat. Add chicken; cook 2 minutes per side. Transfer chicken to plate; set aside.

2. Add onion to skillet; cook and stir 1 minute. Add pepper; cook over medium heat 5 minutes, stirring occasionally. Stir in beans and salsa.

3. Place chicken over bean mixture. Cover; cook 6 to 7 minutes or until chicken is no longer pink in center. Garnish with cilantro.

Makes 4 servings

Chicken and Herb Stew

½ cup all-purpose flour
½ teaspoon salt
¼ teaspoon black pepper
¼ teaspoon paprika
4 chicken drumsticks
4 chicken thighs
2 tablespoons olive oil
12 ounces new potatoes, quartered
2 carrots, quartered lengthwise and
    cut into 3-inch pieces
1 green bell pepper, cut into thin strips
¾ cup chopped onion
2 cloves garlic, minced
1¾ cups water
¼ cup dry white wine
2 chicken bouillon cubes
1 tablespoon chopped fresh oregano
1 teaspoon chopped fresh rosemary
2 tablespoons chopped fresh parsley (optional)

1. Combine flour, salt, black pepper and paprika in shallow dish; stir until well blended. Coat chicken with flour mixture; shake off excess.

2. Heat oil in large skillet over medium-high heat; add chicken. Brown evenly on both sides, turning frequently, about 8 minutes. Remove from skillet; set aside.

3. Add potatoes, carrots, bell pepper, onion and garlic to skillet. Cook and stir 5 minutes or until vegetables are lightly browned. Add water, wine and bouillon. Cook and stir, scraping browned bits from bottom of skillet. Add oregano and rosemary.

4. Stir chicken into vegetable mixture. Cover; simmer 45 to 50 minutes or until chicken is cooked through (165°F), turning occasionally. Garnish with parsley. *Makes 4 servings*

Coconut Curry Chicken Soup

3 cups chicken broth
8 boneless skinless chicken thighs
1 cup chopped onion, divided
1 teaspoon salt, divided
4 whole cloves
1 tablespoon butter
2 tablespoons curry powder
1¼ cups coconut milk
¼ cup plus 1 tablespoon chopped fresh mint, divided
3 tablespoons crystallized ginger
¼ teaspoon ground cloves
1½ cups half-and-half
3 cups cooked rice (optional)
Lime wedges (optional)

1. Bring broth to a boil in large skillet over high heat. Add chicken, ½ cup onion, ½ teaspoon salt and whole cloves. Return to a boil. Reduce heat; cover tightly and simmer 40 minutes or until very tender.

2. Remove chicken; set aside. Reserve 1 cup cooking liquid; discard remaining liquid, onion and cloves. Increase heat to medium-high; melt butter in skillet. Add remaining ½ cup onion; cook and stir 4 minutes or until onion is translucent. Sprinkle curry over onions; cook and stir constantly just until fragrant, about 20 seconds.

3. Add coconut milk, 1 tablespoon mint, ginger, ground cloves and reserved cooking liquid to skillet. Cover; simmer 10 minutes. Add chicken; cover and simmer 15 minutes. Stir in half-and-half and remaining ½ teaspoon salt. Shred chicken slightly, pressing down with a spoon. Cook 1 minute or until heated through. Sprinkle with remaining ¼ cup mint. Spoon rice over each serving and garnish with lime wedges.

Makes 4 servings

Spanish Chicken and Rice

1 tablespoon olive oil
1 pound boneless skinless chicken breasts, diced
1 medium onion, chopped
1 medium red bell pepper, chopped
1 cup chicken broth
1 can (15 ounces) Spanish-style diced tomatoes, undrained
1 cup frozen peas
1 teaspoon garlic powder
1 teaspoon turmeric (optional)
2 cups MINUTE® White Rice, uncooked

Heat oil in large skillet over medium-high heat. Cook chicken, onion and bell pepper until chicken is browned, stirring occasionally.

Add broth, tomatoes, peas, garlic powder and turmeric, if desired; bring to a boil.

Stir in rice. Reduce heat to low; cover. Cook 5 minutes or until rice is tender. *Makes 4 servings*

Homestyle
Skillet Chicken

1 tablespoon Cajun seasoning
½ teaspoon plus ⅛ teaspoon black pepper, divided
½ teaspoon salt, divided
4 chicken thighs
2 tablespoons vegetable oil
4 cloves garlic, minced
8 red or new potatoes, quartered
12 pearl onions, peeled*
1 cup baby carrots
2 stalks celery, halved lengthwise and sliced diagonally into
  ½-inch pieces
½ red bell pepper, diced
2 tablespoons all-purpose flour
1 cup chicken broth
½ cup sherry
2 tablespoons finely chopped fresh parsley

*To peel pearl onions, drop into boiling water for 30 seconds, then plunge immediately into ice water. The peel should slide off.

1. Combine Cajun seasoning, ½ teaspoon black pepper and ¼ teaspoon salt in small bowl. Rub mixture onto all sides of chicken.

2. Heat oil in large heavy skillet over medium-high heat. Add garlic and chicken; cook until chicken is browned, about 3 minutes per side. Transfer chicken to plate; set aside.

3. Add potatoes, onions, carrots, celery and bell pepper to skillet. Cook and stir 3 minutes. Sprinkle flour over vegetables; stir to coat. Slowly stir in broth and sherry, scraping up browned bits from bottom of skillet. Bring mixture to a boil, stirring constantly.

4. Reduce heat to medium-low. Return chicken to skillet. Cover; cook about 30 minutes or until chicken is cooked through (165°F). Increase heat to medium-high; cook uncovered, about 5 minutes or until sauce is thickened.

5. Season with remaining ¼ teaspoon salt and ⅛ teaspoon black pepper. Sprinkle with parsley. *Makes 4 servings*

15-Minute Chicken and Broccoli Risotto

1 tablespoon vegetable oil
1 onion, chopped
2 packages (about 9 ounces each) ready-to-serve yellow rice
2 cups frozen chopped broccoli
1 package (about 6 ounces) refrigerated fully cooked chicken breast strips, cut into pieces
½ cup chicken broth
Sliced almonds (optional)

1. Heat oil in large skillet over medium-high heat. Add onion; cook and stir 3 minutes or until translucent.

2. Knead rice in bag. Add rice, broccoli, chicken and broth to skillet. Cover; cook 6 to 8 minutes or until heated through, stirring occasionally. Garnish with almonds.   *Makes 4 servings*

Chicken Parmesan

Prep Time: 5 minutes • **Cook Time:** 15 minutes • **Stand Time:** 5 minutes

1 tablespoon olive oil
6 skinless, boneless chicken breast halves
1½ cups PREGO® Traditional Italian Sauce *or* PREGO® Organic Tomato & Basil Italian Sauce
¼ cup grated Parmesan cheese
1½ cups shredded mozzarella cheese (about 6 ounces)

1. Heat the oil in a 12-inch skillet over medium-high heat. Add the chicken and cook for 10 minutes or until it's well browned on both sides.

2. Stir the Italian sauce and **3 tablespoons** Parmesan cheese in the skillet. Reduce the heat to medium. Cover and cook for 5 minutes or until the chicken is cooked through.

3. Sprinkle the mozzarella cheese and remaining Parmesan cheese over the chicken. Let stand for 5 minutes or until the cheese is melted.
                                   Makes 6 servings

Chicken with Rice & Asparagus Pilaf

4 boneless skinless chicken breasts
3 teaspoons poultry seasoning, divided
2 tablespoons olive oil
1 onion, chopped
1 cup uncooked rice
1 clove garlic, minced
2 cups chicken broth
¾ teaspoon salt
1 pound asparagus, trimmed and cut into 2-inch pieces
   (about 3 cups)

1. Sprinkle each chicken breast with ¼ teaspoon poultry seasoning. Heat oil in large skillet over medium-high heat. Cook chicken about 2 minutes on each side. Remove from skillet.

2. Cook and stir onion in same skillet 3 minutes. Add rice and garlic; cook and stir 1 to 2 minutes. Add broth, remaining 2 teaspoons poultry seasoning and salt. Bring to a boil over high heat. Reduce heat to low; cook covered, 5 minutes.

3. Stir in asparagus and chicken. Cook covered, 10 to 12 minutes or until rice is tender and chicken is no longer pink in center.

Makes 4 servings

Chinese Take-Out Style Chicken and Broccoli

2 cloves garlic, minced
1 tablespoon fresh grated ginger
⅛ teaspoon red pepper flakes
12 ounces boneless skinless chicken breasts, cut into 2-inch pieces
1 ounce peanuts
2 teaspoons canola oil, divided
1 onion, cut into ½-inch wedges
1 carrot, thinly sliced
2 cups broccoli florets
1¼ cups chicken broth, divided
1 tablespoon cornstarch
2 garlic cloves, minced
2 tablespoons soy sauce

1. To prepare marinade, combine garlic, ginger and pepper flakes in small bowl. Place chicken in bowl; sprinkle marinade on both sides. Cover; refrigerate 30 minutes, turning occasionally.

2. Heat large nonstick skillet over medium-high heat. Add peanuts and cook 2 minutes or until lightly browned, stirring frequently. Remove from skillet; set aside.

3. Remove chicken from marinade; discard marinade. Add 1 teaspoon oil to skillet, tilting to coat lightly. Add chicken; cook 2 minutes. Set aside on separate plate.

4. Add remaining 1 teaspoon oil to skillet; cook onion and carrot 2 minutes. Add broccoli and ¼ cup broth; bring to a boil over medium-high heat. Cover; cook 2 minutes or until broccoli is crisp-tender.

5. Meanwhile, combine remaining 1 cup broth with cornstarch in small bowl; whisk until cornstarch is completely dissolved. Add cornstarch mixture, chicken and garlic to broccoli mixture. Cook 1 minute or until thickened. Remove from heat, sprinkle with soy sauce and peanuts.

Makes 4 servings

Chicken & Rice
Skillet Dinner

Prep Time: 5 minutes • **Cook Time:** 15 minutes

**4 (1 pound) boneless, skinless chicken breast halves,
   cut into strips**
2 tablespoons oil
2 cups sliced zucchini *or* **1 package (16 ounces) frozen
   vegetable blend**
1 jar (15 ounces) medium salsa (1¼ cups)
¾ cup water
1½ cups instant rice
**1½ cups (6 ounces) SARGENTO® BISTRO® Blends Shredded
   Taco Cheese**

COOK chicken in hot oil in large skillet over medium-high heat 5 minutes
or until cooked through, stirring frequently.

ADD zucchini, salsa and water. Heat to a boil; cover and simmer
5 minutes. Reduce heat; stir in rice. Top with cheese. Cover and cook
5 minutes. *Makes 4 servings*

*Tip

Skillet dinners are a fast and easy way to make a meal. They require just a
few ingredients and use only one pan, making cleanup a breeze and leaving
plenty of time to enjoy your meal.

Bow Tie
Pasta Bowl

3 cups chicken broth
6 ounces uncooked bow tie pasta
⅛ teaspoon dried red pepper flakes
1½ cups cooked diced chicken
1 tomato, diced
1 cup packed spring greens or spinach, coarsely chopped, about 1 ounce total
3 tablespoons chopped basil
⅛ teaspoon salt
1 cup shredded mozzarella cheese
4 teaspoons grated Parmesan cheese

1. Bring broth to boil over high heat in large saucepan; add bow ties and pepper flakes. Return to a boil; reduce heat, cover and simmer 10 minutes or until bow ties are al dente.

2. Add chicken; cook 1 minute. Remove from heat; stir in tomato, greens, basil and salt.

3. Spoon into soup bowls; top evenly with mozzarella and Parmesan.

Makes 4 servings

Serving Suggestion: Serve with fresh slices of melon and iced tea with lemon and fresh mint.

Green Bean, Chicken and Rice Dinner

1 tablespoon vegetable oil
4 small boneless skinless chicken breasts*
2 cups frozen cut green beans, thawed
1¾ cups milk
1 can (10¾ ounces) condensed cream of mushroom soup
¼ teaspoon paprika
¼ teaspoon black pepper
2 cups MINUTE® White Rice, uncooked
½ cup canned French-fried onion rings

Or substitute 12 ounces diced chicken.

Heat oil in large nonstick skillet over medium-high heat. Add chicken; cover. Cook 4 minutes on each side or until cooked through (170°F). Remove chicken from skillet; cover to keep warm.

Add beans, milk, soup and seasonings to skillet; stir. Bring to a boil.

Stir in rice. Top with chicken; cover. Reduce heat to low; cook 5 minutes or until rice is tender. Sprinkle with onion rings.   *Makes 4 servings*

Asian Noodles with Vegetables and Chicken

1 tablespoon vegetable oil
2 cups sliced shiitake or button mushrooms
2 cups snow peas, sliced diagonally in half
2 packages (about 1½ ounces each) garlic and vegetable instant rice noodle soup mix
2 cups boiling water
2 packages (6 ounces each) refrigerated fully cooked chicken breast strips, cut into pieces
¼ teaspoon red pepper flakes
2 tablespoons lime juice
1 tablespoon soy sauce

1. Heat oil in large skillet over medium-high heat. Add mushrooms and snow peas; cook 2 to 3 minutes or until snow peas are crisp-tender. Remove from skillet.

2. Break up noodles from soup mixes. Combine noodles, 1 seasoning packet (reserve remaining seasoning packet for another use, if desired), water, chicken and pepper flakes in skillet; mix well. Cook over medium-high heat 5 to 7 minutes or until thickened.

3. Stir in reserved mushrooms, snow peas, lime juice and soy sauce.

Makes 4 servings

**30-Minute Paella
(p. 42)**

**Spaghetti with Spicy
Clam Sauce (p. 49)**

Cajun-Style Corn with Crayfish (p. 43)

Lemon Shrimp with Black Beans and Rice (p. 48)

Sizzlin' Seafood

Southwestern Tilapia with Rice and Beans

4 tilapia fillets, about 4 ounces each
2 tablespoons all-purpose flour
¼ teaspoon salt, divided
⅛ teaspoon black pepper
6 teaspoons butter, divided
1 package (about 8 ounces) ready-to-serve Spanish rice
1 can (about 15 ounces) black beans, rinsed and drained
1 can (about 14 ounces) diced tomatoes with chiles
¼ teaspoon dried oregano
1 green onion, finely chopped

1. Rinse tilapia and pat dry. Combine flour, ⅛ teaspoon salt and pepper in large resealable food storage bag. Add tilapia and shake to coat.

2. Melt 4 teaspoons butter in large skillet over medium-high heat. Add tilapia; cook 2 minutes per side until golden brown and fish just begins to flake when tested with fork. Remove tilapia from skillet; keep warm.

3. Add remaining 2 teaspoons butter to same skillet. Stir in rice, beans, tomatoes, oregano and remaining ⅛ teaspoon salt. Reduce heat to low; simmer 5 minutes, stirring frequently. Sprinkle with green onion.

4. Place tilapia on top of rice mixture in skillet. Serve directly from skillet.

Makes 4 servings

30-Minute Paella

2 tablespoons olive oil
1 package (about 10 ounces) chicken-flavored rice and vermicelli mix
¼ teaspoon red pepper flakes
3½ cups water
1 package (about 10 ounces) refrigerated fully cooked chicken breast strips, cut into ½-inch pieces
1 package (8 ounces) medium raw shrimp, peeled and deveined
1 cup frozen peas
¼ cup diced roasted red pepper

1. Heat oil in large skillet over medium heat. Add vermicelli mix and pepper flakes; cook and stir 2 minutes or until vermicelli is golden.

2. Add water, chicken, shrimp, peas, roasted red pepper and seasoning packet; bring to a boil. Reduce heat to low. Cover; cook 12 to 15 minutes or until rice is tender, stirring occasionally.   *Makes 6 servings*

*Tip

Shrimp shells can be easily removed with your fingers. Start to peel them off on the side with the legs. Lift the shells up and over, then back around to the legs side.

Cajun-Style Corn with Crayfish

6 ears of corn
1 tablespoon vegetable oil
1 onion, chopped
½ cup chopped green bell pepper
½ cup chopped red bell pepper
1 cup water
1 teaspoon salt
⅛ teaspoon black pepper
⅛ teaspoon ground red pepper
¾ pound crayfish tail meat

1. Cut corn from cobs in two or three layers so that kernels are not left whole. Scrape cobs to remove remaining juice and pulp.

2. Heat oil in large skillet over medium heat. Add onion and bell peppers; cook 5 minutes, stirring occasionally. Add corn, water, salt, black pepper and ground red pepper; bring to a boil. Reduce heat to low; simmer 10 to 15 minutes.

3. Add crayfish; return mixture to a simmer. Cook 3 to 5 minutes or just until crayfish turn opaque.

Makes 6 servings

Scallops with
Black Bean and Stout Sauce

1 can (about 15 ounces) black beans, rinsed, drained and chopped
⅓ cup dark-colored beer, such as porter
2 tablespoons soy sauce
2 tablespoons honey
2 teaspoons hoisin sauce
2 cloves garlic, minced
½ teaspoon salt
¼ teaspoon red pepper flakes
2 tablespoons olive oil
1 red bell pepper, seeded and sliced into thin strips
1½ cups fresh snow peas
1½ cups thinly sliced carrots
1½ pounds sea scallops

1. Combine beans, beer, soy sauce, honey, hoisin sauce, garlic, salt and pepper flakes in blender or food processor; set aside.

2. Heat oil in large nonstick skillet over medium-high heat. Add bell pepper, snow peas and carrots; cook and stir 3 minutes. Add scallops and black bean sauce; cook and stir 6 to 10 minutes or until scallops are opaque and mixture is heated through.   *Makes 8 servings*

Garlic Prawns with Green Onion

Prep Time: 15 minutes • **Cook Time:** 10 minutes

2 tablespoons cooking oil
1 tablespoon LEE KUM KEE® Minced Garlic
8 ounces prawns, deveined and patted dry
2 tablespoons LEE KUM KEE® Soy Sauce
2 red chili peppers, cut into thin strips
2 green onions, chopped
1 tablespoon LEE KUM KEE® Pure Sesame Oil

1. Heat skillet over high heat until hot. Add cooking oil, LEE KUM KEE Minced Garlic, prawns and LEE KUM KEE Soy Sauce; cook and stir until prawns turn pink.

2. Add chili peppers, green onions and LEE KUM KEE Pure Sesame Oil; cook 1 minute. Serve immediately.   *Makes 2 servings*

Shrimp Fried Rice

1 cup MINUTE® White Rice, uncooked
2 tablespoons vegetable oil
¾ cup cooked ham, cubed
¾ cup fresh mushrooms, sliced
½ cup frozen peas
¼ cup green onion, sliced
½ pound medium shrimp, peeled, deveined
3 tablespoons soy sauce
1 egg, lightly beaten

Prepare rice according to package directions.

Heat vegetable oil in large nonstick skillet over medium-high heat. Add ham, mushrooms, peas and green onion. Cook and stir 4 minutes.

Add shrimp; cook and stir 4 minutes or until shrimp turn pink.

Stir in rice, soy sauce and egg. Cook until egg is set, stirring occasionally.
Makes 4 servings

Lemon Shrimp with Black Beans and Rice

1 cup uncooked instant brown rice
⅛ teaspoon ground turmeric
   Nonstick cooking spray
1 pound raw shrimp, peeled and deveined (with tails on)
1½ teaspoons chili powder
½ (15-ounce) can black beans, rinsed and drained
1 poblano pepper *or* **½ green bell pepper, minced**
1½ to 2 teaspoons grated lemon peel
3 tablespoons lemon juice
1½ tablespoons extra-virgin olive oil
   Lemon wedges (optional)

1. Cook rice with turmeric according to package directions.

2. Spray large nonstick skillet with cooking spray; place over medium heat. Add shrimp and chili powder; cook and stir 4 minutes or until shrimp are pink and opaque. Add beans, pepper, lemon peel, lemon juice and oil; cook and stir 1 minute or until heated through.

3. Place rice on serving platter. Spoon shrimp mixture over rice. Garnish with lemon wedges. *Makes 6 servings*

Spaghetti with Spicy Clam Sauce

2 teaspoons olive oil
1 clove garlic, minced
2 tomatoes, cored and chopped
1 cup canned crushed tomatoes
¼ teaspoon red pepper flakes
¼ teaspoon salt
⅛ teaspoon black pepper
1 can (6½ ounces) chopped clams, drained
1 cup cooked whole wheat spaghetti

1. Heat oil in large skillet over medium-low heat. Add garlic. Cook and stir 1 minute or until fragrant.

2. Stir in fresh tomatoes; cook 2 minutes or until pulpy. Add crushed tomatoes, pepper flakes, salt and pepper; cook 2 minutes. Add clams; cook 2 to 3 minutes or until heated through.

3. Divide spaghetti among plates; top with clam sauce.

Makes 3 servings

*Tip

When choosing a skillet, look for one that is heavy and conducts heat evenly with a tight-fitting cover. Skillets range in size from 6 to 12 inches.

Halibut Provençal

Nonstick cooking spray
1 can (28 ounces) diced tomatoes
2 cups fennel, stems and fronds removed, sliced thin and chopped
1 cup finely chopped onion
2 tablespoons minced orange peel
2 teaspoons herbes de Provence*
4 (4-ounce) halibut steaks (½ inch thick)
1 tablespoon olive oil
¼ cup plain dry bread crumbs
1 tablespoon grated Parmesan cheese
2 cloves garlic, minced
1 teaspoon paprika
½ teaspoon black pepper
¼ teaspoon salt
Minced fresh basil (optional)

*Herbes de Provence spice mixes usually contain dried basil, fennel seed, lavender, marjoram, rosemary, sage, summer savory and thyme.

1. Spray large skillet with cooking spray; heat over medium heat. Add tomatoes, fennel, onion, orange peel and herbes de Provence. Cook and stir 10 minutes.

2. Place halibut over vegetables; sprinkle with oil. Combine bread crumbs, cheese, garlic, paprika, pepper and salt in small bowl. Sprinkle over fish. Cover skillet; cook 5 to 6 minutes or until fish just begins to flake when tested with fork. Garnish with basil.   *Makes 4 servings*

Gingered Shrimp and Vegetable Fried Skillet

Nonstick cooking spray
½ pound frozen medium or large shrimp, thawed, peeled and deveined
2 teaspoons minced fresh ginger
3 cloves garlic, minced
2 cups sugar snap peas
1 red or yellow bell pepper, cut into thin 1-inch strips
1 package (8½ ounces) cooked brown rice
3 tablespoons soy sauce
¼ cup chopped fresh cilantro or green onions
1 tablespoon dark sesame oil

1. Spray large nonstick skillet with cooking spray; heat over medium-high heat. Add shrimp, ginger and garlic; cook and stir 1 minute.

2. Add peas and bell pepper; cook and stir 4 minutes or until shrimp are pink and opaque and vegetables are crisp-tender.

3. Stir in rice and soy sauce; cook and stir 2 minutes or until heated through. Turn off heat; stir in cilantro and sesame oil.

Makes 4 servings

Quick Pasta with Peppers
(p. 68)

Couscous Primavera
(p. 83)

Chinese Sweet and Sour Vegetables (p. 82)

Spaghetti Squash Primavera (p. 69)

Meatless Creations

Italian Vegetable Stew

Prep Time: 10 minutes • **Cook Time:** 25 minutes

1 teaspoon olive oil
2 medium zucchini, halved lengthwise and thinly sliced
1 medium eggplant, chopped
1 large onion, thinly sliced
⅛ teaspoon ground black pepper
1 jar (1 pound 10 ounces) RAGÚ® Light Pasta Sauce
3 tablespoons grated Parmesan cheese
1 box (10 ounces) couscous

1. In 12-inch nonstick skillet, heat olive oil over medium heat and cook zucchini, eggplant, onion and pepper, stirring occasionally, 15 minutes or until vegetables are golden.

2. Stir in Pasta Sauce and cheese. Bring to a boil over high heat. Reduce heat to low and simmer covered 10 minutes.

3. Meanwhile, prepare couscous according to package directions. Serve vegetable mixture over hot couscous.   *Makes 4 servings*

Moroccan Supper

Prep Time: 10 minutes • **Cook Time:** 30 minutes

1 (7.2-ounce) package RICE-A-RONI® Rice Pilaf
½ cup chopped onion
2 cloves garlic, minced
2 tablespoons olive oil or margarine
1 teaspoon ground cumin
¼ teaspoon ground cinnamon
1 (15-ounce) can garbanzo beans or chickpeas, rinsed and drained
1½ cups broccoli flowerets
¼ cup dried apricots, slivered
⅓ cup slivered almonds, toasted
¼ cup chopped cilantro (optional)

1. In large skillet over medium heat, sauté rice-pasta mix, onion and garlic with oil until pasta is light golden brown.

2. Slowly stir in 2 cups water, cumin, cinnamon and Special Seasonings; bring to a boil. Cover; reduce heat to low. Simmer 10 minutes.

3. Stir in beans, broccoli and apricots. Cover; simmer 10 to 12 minutes or until rice is tender. Serve topped with almonds and cilantro, if desired.

Makes 4 servings

Variation: For a Southwestern flair, use black beans, 1½ cups corn and ¼ teaspoon chili powder instead of garbanzo beans, apricots and cinnamon.

Pasta with Fresh Tomato-Olive Sauce

2 tablespoons olive oil
1 onion, chopped
2 cloves garlic, minced
4 tomatoes, seeded and chopped (about 3 cups)
¾ teaspoon dried oregano
⅛ teaspoon red pepper flakes
⅔ cup chopped pitted kalamata olives
1 tablespoon capers
   Salt and black pepper
1 package (16 ounces) uncooked spaghetti
   Grated Parmesan cheese

1. Heat oil in large skillet over medium heat. Add onion and garlic; cook and stir about 4 minutes or until onion is tender.

2. Add tomatoes, oregano and pepper flakes; simmer uncovered, 15 to 20 minutes or until sauce is thickened. Stir in olives, capers, salt and black pepper.

3. Meanwhile, cook spaghetti according to package directions; drain. Add spaghetti to skillet; toss to coat with sauce. Sprinkle with cheese before serving.   *Makes 6 to 8 servings*

*Tip

If your skillet is not large enough to hold both the sauce and the cooked spaghetti, toss them together in a heated serving bowl.

Spring Vegetable Ragoût

1 tablespoon olive oil
2 leeks, thinly sliced
3 cloves garlic, minced
1 cup vegetable broth
1 package (10 ounces) frozen corn
½ pound yellow squash, halved lengthwise and cut into
   ½-inch pieces (about 1¼ cups)
1 bag (6 ounces) frozen edamame (soybeans), pods removed
1 bag (4 ounces) shredded carrots
3 cups cherry tomatoes, halved
1 teaspoon dried tarragon
1 teaspoon dried basil
1 teaspoon dried oregano
   Salt and black pepper
   Minced fresh parsley (optional)

1. Heat oil in large skillet over medium heat. Add leeks and garlic; cook and stir just until fragrant. Add broth, corn, squash, edamame and carrots; cook and stir until squash is tender.

2. Add tomatoes, tarragon, basil and oregano; stir well. Reduce heat and simmer covered, 2 minutes or until tomatoes are soft.

3. Season with salt and pepper. Garnish with parsley.

Makes 6 servings

Hot Three-Bean Casserole

2 tablespoons olive oil
1 cup coarsely chopped onions
1 cup chopped celery
2 cloves garlic, minced
1 can (about 15 ounces) chickpeas, rinsed and drained
1 can (about 15 ounces) kidney beans, rinsed and drained
1 cup coarsely chopped tomato
1 can (about 8 ounces) tomato sauce
1 cup water
1 to 2 jalapeño peppers,* minced
1 tablespoon chili powder
2 teaspoons sugar
1½ teaspoons ground cumin
1 teaspoon salt
1 teaspoon dried oregano
¼ teaspoon black pepper
2½ cups (10 ounces) frozen cut green beans
Fresh oregano (optional)

Jalapeño peppers can sting and irritate the skin, so wear rubber gloves when handling peppers and do not touch your eyes.

1. Heat oil in large skillet over medium heat. Add onions, celery and garlic; cook and stir 5 minutes or until onions are translucent.

2. Add chickpeas, kidney beans, tomato, tomato sauce, water, jalapeños, chili powder, sugar, cumin, salt, dried oregano and black pepper; bring to a boil. Reduce heat and simmer uncovered, 20 minutes. Add green beans. Simmer uncovered, 10 minutes or until beans are tender. Garnish with fresh oregano. *Makes 12 servings*

Skillet Vegetable Lasagna

Prep Time: 10 minutes • **Cook Time:** 15 minutes

1¾ cups SWANSON® Vegetable Broth (Regular or Certified Organic)

⅔ of a 1-pound package of uncooked oven-ready (no-boil) lasagna noodles (about 15)

1 can (10¾ ounces) CAMPBELL'S® Condensed Cream of Mushroom Soup (Regular or 98% Fat Free)

1 can (about 14.5 ounces) diced tomatoes, undrained

1 package (10 ounces) frozen chopped spinach, thawed and well drained

1 cup ricotta cheese

1 cup shredded mozzarella cheese (about 4 ounces)

1. Heat the broth in a 12-inch skillet over medium-high heat to a boil. Break the noodles into pieces and add to the broth. Reduce the heat to low. Cook for 3 minutes or until the noodles are tender.

2. Stir the soup, tomatoes and spinach in the skillet. Cook for 5 minutes or until the mixture is hot and bubbling.

3. Remove the skillet from the heat. Spoon the ricotta cheese on top and sprinkle with the mozzarella cheese.   *Makes 4 servings*

Kitchen Tip: You can try using 4 ounces mozzarella, cut into very thin slices, instead of the shredded mozzarella.

Quick Pasta
with Peppers

8 ounces uncooked penne or rigatoni pasta
2 tablespoons olive oil
1 *each* red, yellow and green bell pepper, thinly sliced
1 jar (about 26 ounces) marinara sauce
¼ cup grated Parmesan cheese

1. Cook penne according to package directions; drain and keep warm.

2. Meanwhile, heat oil in large skillet over medium-high heat. Add bell peppers; cook 2 minutes, stirring frequently. Reduce heat to medium-low; stir in sauce. Cook and stir 5 minutes over medium heat, stirring frequently.

3. Pour sauce over hot penne; sprinkle with cheese before serving.

Makes 6 to 8 servings

Easy Skillet Ravioli

Prep Time: 5 minutes • **Cook Time:** 20 minutes

1 package (about 26 ounces) frozen cheese ravioli
2¼ cups water
½ teaspoon salt
1 jar (1 pound 10 ounces) RAGÚ® Chunky Pasta Sauce
¼ cup heavy cream, half-and-half, evaporated milk, milk or nondairy creamer (optional)

1. In 12-inch nonstick skillet, bring ravioli, water and salt to a boil over high heat. Continue boiling, stirring gently to separate ravioli, 5 minutes.

2. Stir in Pasta Sauce. Cook covered over medium heat, stirring occasionally, 10 minutes or until ravioli are tender. Stir in cream and heat through. Garnish, if desired, with grated Parmesan cheese.

Makes 4 servings

Spaghetti Squash Primavera

1 teaspoon olive oil
¼ cup sliced mushrooms
¼ cup sliced green onions
¼ cup diced zucchini
¼ cup diced carrot
¼ cup diced green bell pepper
2 cloves garlic, minced
1 plum tomato, diced
1 tablespoon red wine or water
½ teaspoon dried basil
¼ teaspoon salt
⅛ teaspoon black pepper
2 cups cooked spaghetti squash (about 2 pounds)
2 tablespoons freshly grated Parmesan cheese

1. Heat oil in medium skillet over low heat. Add mushrooms, green onions, zucchini, carrot, bell pepper and garlic; cook 10 to 12 minutes or until crisp-tender, stirring occasionally. Stir in tomato, wine, basil, salt and black pepper; cook 4 to 5 minutes, stirring once or twice.

2. Serve vegetables over spaghetti squash. Top with cheese.

Makes 2 servings

Penne with Creamy Tomato Sauce

1 tablespoon olive or vegetable oil
½ cup diced onion
2 tablespoons dry vermouth, white wine or chicken broth
1 can (14.5 ounces) CONTADINA® Recipe Ready Diced Tomatoes with Italian Herbs, undrained
½ cup heavy whipping cream
8 ounces dry penne or rigatoni, cooked, drained, kept warm
1 cup pitted ripe olives, drained, sliced
½ cup (2 ounces) grated Parmesan cheese
¼ cup sliced green onions

1. Heat oil in large skillet. Add diced onion; sauté 2 to 3 minutes or until onion is tender.

2. Add vermouth; cook 1 minute.

3. Stir in undrained tomatoes, cream, pasta, olives and Parmesan cheese; heat thoroughly, stirring occasionally. Sprinkle with green onions.

Makes 4 servings

*Tip

If the pasta sticks together after cooking, toss it very briefly with hot running water. Make sure you drain it thoroughly, as excess cooking water will dilute the sauce.

Szechuan Vegetable Lo Mein

Prep and Cook Time: 20 minutes

2 cans (about 14 ounces each) vegetable broth
2 teaspoons minced garlic
1 teaspoon minced fresh ginger
¼ teaspoon red pepper flakes
1 package (16 ounces) frozen vegetable medley, such as broccoli, carrots, water chestnuts and red bell peppers
1 package (5 ounces) Asian curly noodles or 5 ounces uncooked angel hair pasta, broken in half
3 tablespoons soy sauce
1 tablespoon dark sesame oil
¼ cup thinly sliced green onions

1. Combine broth, garlic, ginger and pepper flakes in large deep skillet. Cover and bring to a boil over high heat.

2. Add vegetables and noodles to skillet; cover and return to a boil. Reduce heat to medium-low; simmer uncovered, 5 to 6 minutes or until vegetables and noodles are tender, stirring occasionally.

3. Stir in soy sauce and oil; cook 3 minutes. Stir in green onions; ladle into bowls. *Makes 4 servings*

Note: For a heartier main dish, add 1 package drained (about 14 ounces) extra firm tofu, cut into ¾-inch pieces, to the broth mixture with the soy sauce and sesame oil.

Fire & Ice
Brunch Skillet

Prep Time: 5 minutes • **Cook Time:** 30 minutes

1 (6.8-ounce) package RICE-A-RONI® Spanish Rice
2 tablespoons butter or margarine
1 (16-ounce) jar salsa
⅓ cup sour cream
¼ cup thinly sliced green onions
4 large eggs
1 cup (4 ounces) shredded Cheddar cheese
Chopped cilantro (optional)

1. In large skillet over medium heat, sauté rice-vermicelli mix with butter until vermicelli is golden brown.

2. Slowly stir in 2 cups water, salsa and Special Seasonings; bring to a boil. Reduce heat to low. Cover; simmer 15 to 20 minutes or until rice is tender.

3. Stir in sour cream and green onions. Using large spoon, make 4 indentations in rice mixture. Break 1 egg into each indentation. Reduce heat to low. Cover; cook 8 minutes or until eggs are cooked to desired doneness.

4. Sprinkle cheese evenly over eggs and rice. Cover; let stand 3 minutes or until cheese is melted. Sprinkle with cilantro, if desired.

Makes 4 servings

Pasta
Primavera

8 ounces uncooked linguine
1 tablespoon butter
2 green onions, sliced diagonally
1 clove garlic, minced
1 cup fresh mushroom slices
1 cup broccoli florets
2½ cups fresh snow peas
4 to 8 asparagus spears, cut into 2-inch pieces
1 red bell pepper, cut into thin strips
½ cup evaporated milk
½ teaspoon dried tarragon
½ teaspoon black pepper
⅓ cup grated Parmesan cheese

1. Cook linguine according to package directions. Drain; set aside.

2. Melt butter in large nonstick skillet. Add green onions and garlic; cook over medium heat until softened. Add mushrooms and broccoli. Cover; cook 3 minutes or until mushrooms are tender. Add snow peas, asparagus, bell pepper, evaporated milk, tarragon and black pepper. Cook and stir until vegetables are crisp-tender and lightly coated.

3. Add cheese and linguine; toss to coat.   *Makes 4 servings*

Winter Squash Risotto

2 tablespoons olive oil
2 cups butternut squash, peeled and cut into 1-inch pieces
1 shallot or onion, finely chopped
½ teaspoon paprika
¼ teaspoon salt
¼ teaspoon dried thyme
¼ teaspoon black pepper
1 cup arborio rice
¼ cup dry white wine (optional)
4 to 5 cups hot vegetable broth
½ cup grated Parmesan or Romano cheese

1. Heat oil in large skillet over medium heat. Add squash; cook and stir 3 minutes. Add shallot; cook 3 to 4 minutes or until squash is almost tender. Stir in paprika, salt, thyme and pepper. Add rice; stir to coat with oil.

2. Add wine, if desired; cook and stir until wine evaporates. Reduce heat to low. Add ½ cup broth; cook over medium heat, stirring occasionally. When rice is almost dry, stir in another ½ cup broth. Continue to stir rice occasionally, adding ½ cup broth each time previous addition is absorbed. Rice is done when consistency is creamy and grains are tender with slight resistance. (Total cooking time will be 20 to 30 minutes.)

3. Sprinkle with cheese. Serve immediately.　　　*Makes 4 to 6 servings*

Pasta with Spinach and Ricotta

Prep and Cook Time: 24 minutes

8 ounces uncooked tri-colored rotini pasta
Nonstick cooking spray
1 package (10 ounces) frozen chopped spinach, thawed and squeezed dry
2 teaspoons minced garlic
1 cup ricotta cheese
½ cup water
3 tablespoons grated Parmesan cheese, divided
Salt and black pepper

1. Cook rotini according to package directions. Drain well; cover and keep warm.

2. Spray large skillet with cooking spray; heat over medium-low heat. Add spinach and garlic; cook and stir 5 minutes. Stir in ricotta, water and 1½ tablespoons Parmesan. Season with salt and pepper.

3. Add rotini to skillet; stir until well blended. Sprinkle with remaining 1½ tablespoons Parmesan. *Makes 4 servings*

Chinese Sweet and Sour Vegetables

3 cups broccoli florets
2 carrots, diagonally sliced
1 red bell pepper, cut into short, thin strips
¼ cup water
2 teaspoons cornstarch
1 teaspoon sugar
⅓ cup unsweetened pineapple juice
1 tablespoon rice vinegar
1 tablespoon soy sauce
½ teaspoon dark sesame oil
¼ cup chopped fresh cilantro (optional)

1. Combine broccoli, carrots, bell pepper and water in large skillet; bring to a boil over high heat. Reduce heat to medium. Cover and steam 4 minutes or until vegetables are crisp-tender. Drain.

2. Meanwhile, combine cornstarch and sugar in small bowl. Blend in pineapple juice, vinegar and soy sauce until smooth.

3. Add to skillet; cook and stir 2 minutes or until sauce boils and thickens. Return vegetables to skillet; toss with sauce. Stir in oil. Garnish with cilantro. *Makes 4 servings*

Couscous Primavera

Nonstick cooking spray
1 shallot, minced *or* **¼ cup minced red onion**
**8 spears fresh asparagus, cooked and cut into
    1-inch pieces**
1 cup frozen peas
1 cup halved grape tomatoes
½ cup water
⅛ teaspoon salt
⅛ teaspoon black pepper
6 tablespoons uncooked whole wheat couscous
¼ cup grated Parmesan cheese

1. Spray large skillet with cooking spray. Add shallot; cook over medium-high heat 3 minutes or until tender. Add asparagus and peas; cook 2 minutes or until peas are heated through. Add tomatoes; cook 2 minutes or until softened. Add water, salt and pepper; bring to a boil.

2. Stir in couscous. Reduce heat to low; cover and simmer 2 minutes or until liquid is absorbed. Fluff with fork and stir in cheese. Serve immediately.
Makes 2 servings

Penne
Puttanesca

Prep Time: 10 minutes • **Cook Time:** 10 minutes

Vegetable cooking spray
½ **cup kalamata olives, drained, pitted and chopped**
1 **tablespoon capers, drained**
¼ **teaspoon crushed red pepper**
2 **cups PREGO® Tomato, Basil & Garlic Italian Sauce**
¼ **cup grated Parmesan cheese**
½ **of a 16-ounce package tube-shaped pasta (penne), cooked
and drained**

1. Spray a 10-inch skillet with cooking spray. Heat over medium-high heat for 1 minute. Add the olives, capers and red pepper. Cook for 2 minutes, stirring often. Stir the sauce and 2 tablespoons of the cheese into the skillet. Heat to a boil.

2. Stir the pasta into the skillet. Heat, stirring occasionally, until hot and bubbling. Top with the remaining cheese.   *Makes 4 servings*

*Tip

Capers are the small-pea-sized buds of a flower from the caper bush. Found mostly in Central America and the Mediterranean, capers add pungency to sauces. Usually, these green buds are pickled and can be found in the condiment section of the supermarket. They taste very much like gherkin pickles.

Two Cheese Mediterranean Skillet

6 ounces uncooked penne pasta
2 tablespoons olive oil, divided
4 cloves garlic, minced
2 cups diced eggplant
1½ cups matchstick-size zucchini strips
1 green bell pepper, cut into 1-inch pieces
1 cup chopped onion
½ pound mushrooms, cut into quarters
1½ teaspoons dried basil
¾ teaspoon salt
⅛ teaspoon black pepper
4 plum tomatoes, cut into quarters and seeded
2 to 3 tablespoons capers, well-drained (optional)
3 ounces provolone cheese, shredded
¼ cup grated Parmesan cheese, divided

1. Cook penne according to package directions.

2. Meanwhile, heat 1 tablespoon oil in large nonstick skillet over medium-high heat 1 minute. Add garlic; cook 1 minute. Add eggplant, zucchini, bell pepper, onion, mushrooms, basil, salt and black pepper. Cook 15 minutes or until eggplant is tender.

3. Gently stir in tomatoes and capers, if desired. Reduce heat; cover and simmer 5 minutes.

4. Remove skillet from heat; toss with remaining 1 tablespoon oil, provolone and 2 tablespoons Parmesan.

5. Place cooked penne on serving platter. Spoon vegetable mixture over penne and top with remaining 2 tablespoons Parmesan.

Makes 4 servings

Southern Pork Barbecue Dinner (p. 101)

Pork and Sweet Potato Skillet (p. 94)

Hearty Pork, Apple and Noodle Skillet (p. 100)

Sautéed Pork & Cheddar Studded Wild Rice (p. 95)

Pleasing **Pork**

Country Skillet Hash

Prep Time: 10 minutes • **Cook Time:** 15 minutes

2 tablespoons butter or margarine
4 boneless pork chops (¾ inch thick), diced
¼ teaspoon black pepper
¼ teaspoon cayenne pepper (optional)
1 medium onion, chopped
2 cloves garlic, minced
1 can (14½ ounces) DEL MONTE® Whole New Potatoes, drained and diced
1 can (14½ ounces) DEL MONTE® Original Recipe Stewed Tomatoes, undrained*
1 medium green bell pepper, chopped
½ teaspoon thyme, crushed

*May substitute DEL MONTE Diced Tomatoes, undrained

1. Melt butter in large skillet over medium heat. Add meat; cook, stirring occasionally, until no longer pink in center. Season with black pepper and cayenne pepper, if desired.

2. Add onion and garlic; cook until tender. Stir in potatoes, tomatoes, green pepper and thyme. Cook 5 minutes, stirring frequently. Season with salt, if desired. *Makes 4 servings*

*Tip
This hash may be topped with a poached or fried egg.

Pork & Rice Provençal

Prep Time: 10 minutes • **Cook Time:** 40 minutes

4 well-trimmed boneless pork loin chops, ¾-inch thick (about 1 pound)
1 teaspoon dried basil
½ teaspoon dried thyme
½ teaspoon garlic salt
¼ teaspoon ground black pepper
2 tablespoons butter or margarine, divided
1 (6.8-ounce) package RICE-A-RONI® Beef Flavor
½ cup chopped onion
1 clove garlic, minced
1 (14½-ounce) can seasoned diced tomatoes, undrained
1 (2¼-ounce) can sliced ripe olives, drained *or* ⅓ cup sliced pitted kalamata olives

1. Sprinkle pork chops with basil, thyme, garlic salt and pepper; set aside. In large skillet over medium-high heat, melt 1 tablespoon butter. Add pork chops; cook 3 minutes. Reduce heat to medium; turn pork chops over and cook 3 minutes. Remove from skillet; set aside.

2. In same skillet over medium heat, sauté rice-vermicelli mix, onion and garlic with remaining 1 tablespoon butter until vermicelli is golden brown.

3. Slowly stir in 1¾ cups water, tomatoes and Special Seasonings; bring to a boil. Cover; reduce heat to low. Simmer 10 minutes.

4. Add pork chops and olives. Cover; simmer 10 minutes or until rice is tender and pork chops are no longer pink inside.   *Makes 4 servings*

Pork and Sweet Potato Skillet

Prep Time: 20 minutes • **Cook Time:** 12 to 15 minutes

- **¾ pound pork tenderloin, cut into 1-inch cubes**
- **1 tablespoon plus 1 teaspoon butter, divided**
- **¼ teaspoon salt**
- **⅛ teaspoon black pepper**
- **2 sweet potatoes, peeled and cut into ½-inch pieces (about 2 cups)**
- **1 onion, sliced**
- **¼ pound smoked turkey sausage, halved lengthwise and cut into ½-inch pieces**
- **1 red apple, cored and cut into ½-inch pieces**
- **½ cup prepared sweet-and-sour sauce**
- **2 tablespoons chopped fresh parsley (optional)**

1. Place pork and 1 teaspoon butter to large nonstick skillet; cook and stir 2 to 3 minutes over medium-high heat or until pork is no longer pink. Season with salt and pepper. Remove from skillet.

2. Add remaining 1 tablespoon butter, potatoes and onion to skillet. Cover; cook and stir over medium-low heat 8 to 10 minutes or until tender.

3. Add pork, sausage, apple and sweet-and-sour sauce to skillet; cook and stir until heated through. Garnish with parsley.   *Makes 4 servings*

Sautéed Pork & Cheddar Studded Wild Rice

Prep Time: 20 minutes • **Cook Time:** 15 minutes

- ¼ **teaspoon cinnamon**
- 1 **pound boneless pork loin, sliced ¼-inch thick**
- 1 **tablespoon corn or canola oil**
- 1 **medium onion, chopped**
- 2 **cups apple juice**
- 1 **package (6.5 ounces) quick-cooking long grain and wild rice mix**
- ½ **cup sweetened dried cranberries**
- 1½ **cups (6 ounces) SARGENTO® ARTISAN BLENDS™ Shredded Double Cheddar Cheese, divided**

SPRINKLE cinnamon over pork loin slices. Heat oil in large skillet over medium heat. Cook pork in skillet 5 minutes on each side or until lightly browned and cooked through. Remove meat from skillet and set aside; keep warm.

PLACE onion in skillet and cook over medium heat 4 minutes or just until onion is softened. Add apple juice and rice mix (including seasoning packet, if provided); heat to a boil. Stir in cranberries; cover. Remove from heat; let stand 7 minutes.

STIR 1 cup cheese into rice mixture. Arrange meat slices over rice and cheese mixture; top with remaining cheese. Cover skillet and heat over medium heat 3 minutes or until cheese is melted.   *Makes 6 servings*

Aloha Pork Chop Skillet

      1 tablespoon vegetable oil
      4 pork chops
      1 medium red bell pepper, cut into chunks
      1 medium yellow bell pepper, cut into chunks
      2 cans (8 ounces each) pineapple chunks in juice, undrained
      ½ cup fat-free reduced-sodium chicken broth
      ¼ cup sweet-and-sour sauce
   1½ teaspoons garlic powder
      2 cups MINUTE® White Rice, uncooked

Heat oil in large nonstick skillet over medium-high heat. Add chops; cook 5 minutes on each side or until browned. Remove chops; cover to keep warm.

Add bell peppers, pineapple, broth, sauce and garlic powder to skillet; mix well. Bring to a boil.

Stir in rice. Top with chops; cover. Reduce heat to medium-low; simmer 5 minutes or until chops are cooked through (160°F). Remove from heat; let stand 5 minutes.   *Makes 4 servings*

Country Pork Skillet

      4 boneless top loin pork chops, diced
      1 (12-ounce) jar pork gravy
      2 tablespoons ketchup
      8 small red potatoes, diced
      2 cups frozen mixed vegetables

In large skillet, brown pork cubes; stir in gravy, ketchup and potatoes; cover and simmer for 10 minutes. Stir in vegetables; cook for 10 to 15 minutes longer or until vegetables are tender.   *Makes 4 servings*

Favorite recipe from **National Pork Board**

Ham and Swiss Penne Skillet

6 ounces uncooked penne pasta
2 slices bread, torn into pieces
5 tablespoons butter, divided
3 tablespoons all-purpose flour
2¾ cups milk
1 cup frozen corn, thawed
¾ cup frozen peas, thawed
6 ounces ham, diced
1 cup (4 ounces) shredded Swiss cheese
½ cup finely chopped green onions
   Salt and black pepper

1. Cook penne according to package directions. Drain well; keep warm.

2. Place bread in food processor; pulse to form coarse crumbs. Melt 2 tablespoons butter in large skillet over medium heat. Add bread crumbs; cook and stir 2 minutes or until golden. Transfer to plate; set aside.

3. Melt remaining 3 tablespoons butter in same skillet over medium heat. Add flour; whisk 2 minutes or until smooth. Gradually add milk, whisking constantly to blend. Cook and stir 4 minutes or until slightly thickened. Add penne, corn, peas, ham, cheese and green onions; stir gently to blend. Season with salt and pepper. Cook 4 minutes or until heated through. Sprinkle with bread crumbs. Serve immediately.   *Makes 4 servings*

Hearty Pork, Apple and Noodle Skillet

2 apples, such as Fuji or Golden Delicious, peeled and cored
2 tablespoons butter, divided
1 onion, finely chopped
1 package (about 27 ounces) garlic and herb marinated pork loin fillet
1½ cups chicken broth
½ cup milk
1 package (about 4 ounces) stroganoff pasta mix
¼ teaspoon black pepper
¼ cup sour cream

1. Cut apples into ¼-inch-thick slices. Melt 1 tablespoon butter in large nonstick skillet over medium heat. Add apples and onion; cook 5 to 10 minutes or until apples are lightly browned. Remove to small bowl; set aside.

2. Cut half of pork loin into ½-inch-thick slices. (Reserve remaining pork for another meal.) Melt remaining 1 tablespoon butter in skillet over medium heat. Brown pork in batches, 2 to 3 minutes per side. *Do not overcook.* Remove to plate; set aside.

3. Place broth and milk in skillet; bring to a boil. Add pasta mix, apple mixture and pepper; mix well. Cook over medium heat 10 minutes or until noodles are tender and sauce is slightly thickened. Stir in sour cream. Serve pork over noodles. *Makes 4 servings*

Southern Pork Barbecue Dinner

    1 tablespoon vegetable oil
    ½ cup chopped onion
    ½ cup chopped celery
    ½ cup chopped green bell pepper
    1 container (about 18 ounces) refrigerated fully cooked
       shredded pork
    1 can (about 15 ounces) pinto beans or black-eyed peas,
       rinsed and drained
    1 can (about 8 ounces) tomato sauce
    2 tablespoons Dijon mustard

1. Heat oil in large skillet over medium-high heat. Add onion, celery and bell pepper; cook and stir 5 minutes or until tender.

2. Reduce heat to low. Stir in pork, beans, tomato sauce and mustard; cook 5 to 10 minutes or until heated through.   *Makes 4 to 6 servings*

Spanish Pork Chops

Prep Time: 5 minutes • **Cook Time:** 30 minutes

    4 pork chops (about 1 pound)
    1 (6.8-ounce) package RICE-A-RONI® Spanish Rice
    2 tablespoons butter or margarine
    1 (14½-ounce) can diced tomatoes, undrained

1. In large skillet over medium-high heat, brown pork chops 3 minutes on each side; set aside.

2. In same skillet, sauté rice-vermicelli with butter until vermicelli is golden brown.

3. Slowly stir in 2¼ cups water, tomatoes and Special Seasonings; bring to a boil. Reduce heat to low. Cover; simmer 10 minutes.

4. Add pork chops; return to a simmer. Cover; simmer 8 to 10 minutes or until rice is tender and pork chops are no longer pink inside.

Makes 4 servings

Pork Chop Skillet Dinner

Prep Time: 10 minutes • **Cook Time:** 40 minutes

1 tablespoon olive oil or vegetable oil
4 bone-in pork chops, ¾-inch thick
1 medium onion, chopped (about ½ cup)
1 cup uncooked regular long-grain white rice
1 can (10½ ounces) CAMPBELL'S® Condensed Chicken Broth
1 cup orange juice
3 tablespoons chopped fresh parsley
4 orange slices

1. Heat the oil in a 10-inch skillet over medium-high heat. Add the pork and cook until it's well browned on both sides.

2. Add the onion and rice to the skillet and cook and stir until the rice is browned. Stir in the broth, orange juice and 2 tablespoons parsley and heat to a boil. Reduce the heat to low. Cover and cook for 20 minutes or until the pork is cooked through and the rice is tender.

3. Top with the orange slices and sprinkle with the remaining parsley.

Makes 4 servings

Kitchen Tip: Serve with a tossed green salad. For dessert, serve chunky applesauce.

Herbed Beef & Vegetable Skillet
(p. 133)

Hearty Chili Macaroni
(p. 114)

Five-Spice Beef Skillet
(p. 132)

Asian Basil Beef and Rice
(p. 115)

Sensational Beef

Cheeseburger Pasta

Prep Time: 5 minutes • **Cook Time:** 20 minutes

1 pound ground beef
1 can (10¾ ounces) CAMPBELL'S® Condensed Cheddar Cheese Soup
1 can (10¾ ounces) CAMPBELL'S® Condensed Tomato Soup (Regular or Healthy Request®)
1½ cups water
2 cups uncooked medium shell-shaped pasta

1. Cook the beef in a 10-inch skillet over medium-high heat until it's well browned, stirring often to separate meat. Pour off any fat.

2. Stir the soups, water and pasta in the skillet and heat to a boil. Reduce the heat to medium. Cook for 10 minutes or until the pasta is tender, stirring often.   *Makes 5 servings*

Serving Suggestion: Serve with carrot and celery sticks with Ranch dressing for dipping. For dessert, serve store bought brownies topped with vanilla ice cream.

Mexican Linguine

Prep Time: 5 minutes • **Start to Finish:** 15 minutes

1 pound lean ground beef
1 small onion, chopped
1 jar (16 ounces) ORTEGA® Garden Vegetable Salsa
1 cup whole-kernel corn
¾ cup water
1 packet (1.25 ounces) ORTEGA® Taco Seasoning Mix
1 pound linguine pasta
½ cup (2 ounces) shredded Cheddar cheese

Cook and stir beef and onion in large skillet until beef is browned and onion is tender.

Stir in salsa, corn, water and seasoning mix. Cook and stir over medium heat until thickened.

Cook pasta according to package directions. Toss cooked pasta with meat mixture and top with cheese. *Makes 4 servings*

*Tip

Try different pastas, including macaroni, shells, wagon wheels or other easy-to-eat shapes.

Beef with Snow Peas & Baby Corn

¾ **pound ground beef**
1 **clove garlic, minced**
1 **teaspoon vegetable oil**
6 **ounces snow peas, halved lengthwise**
1 **red bell pepper, cut into strips**
1 **can (15 ounces) baby corn, drained and rinsed**
1 **tablespoon soy sauce**
1 **teaspoon sesame oil**
   Salt and black pepper
2 **cups cooked rice**

1. Cook beef and garlic 6 to 8 minutes in large skillet over medium-high heat, stirring to break up meat. Drain fat. Set aside.

2. Heat vegetable oil in skillet over medium-high heat. Add snow peas and bell pepper; cook and stir 2 to 3 minutes or until vegetables are crisp-tender. Stir in beef mixture, baby corn, soy sauce and sesame oil; cook until heated through. Season with salt and black pepper. Serve over rice.

Makes 4 servings

Skillet Franks
and Potatoes

Hands On: 40 minutes • **Total Time:** 40 minutes

- **1 package (16 ounces each) HEBREW NATIONAL® Quarter Pound Dinner Beef Franks**
- **3 tablespoons PURE WESSON® Vegetable Oil, divided**
- **4 medium red potatoes, chopped, cooked and drained (about 3 cups)**
- **1 large onion, chopped (about 1 cup)**
- **1 medium green bell pepper, chopped (about 1 cup)**
- **1 teaspoon ground dried sage**
- **½ teaspoon salt**
- **¼ teaspoon ground black pepper**
- **2 tablespoons chopped fresh parsley (optional)**

Make shallow cuts in franks (no more than halfway through) about every inch. Heat 1 tablespoon of the oil in large nonstick skillet over medium heat. Add franks; heat 5 minutes or until browned, turning occasionally. Remove franks from skillet; set aside.

Add the remaining 2 tablespoons oil, potatoes, onion and bell pepper to same skillet. Cook and stir 12 minutes or until potatoes are golden brown. Stir in sage, salt and pepper; mix well.

Return franks to skillet. Cook 5 minutes or until heated through, turning franks once halfway through cooking time. Sprinkle with parsley, if desired. *Makes 4 servings*

Hearty Chili
Macaroni

Hands On: 20 minutes • **Total Time:** 20 minutes

8 ounces dry small elbow macaroni, uncooked (2 cups)
1 pound ground sirloin
1 medium onion, chopped (about ½ cup)
1 can (15 ounces) red kidney beans, drained, rinsed
1 can (14.5 ounces) HUNT'S® Petite Diced Tomatoes with Mild
**   Green Chilies, undrained**
1 package (1.25 ounces) chili seasoning mix
1½ teaspoons granulated sugar

1. Cook macaroni according to package directions.

2. Brown meat with onion in a large skillet over medium-high heat while cooking macaroni; drain. Add beans, tomatoes with their liquid, the chili seasoning and sugar; stir until well blended. Bring to a boil; cover. Reduce heat to low; simmer 10 minutes, stirring occasionally.

3. Drain macaroni; stir into meat mixture.   *Makes 6 servings*

*Tip
Kidney beans can be used interchangeably with pinto beans and are available dried and canned.

Asian Basil Beef and Rice

1 package (about 17 ounces) refrigerated fully cooked beef pot roast in gravy or beef tips in gravy
1 tablespoon vegetable oil
2 cups sliced mushrooms
1 pouch (about 9 ounces) teriyaki-flavored ready-to-serve rice
2 tablespoons water
1 tablespoon hoisin sauce or Asian chili garlic sauce
1 teaspoon soy sauce
1 tablespoon sliced green onion
1 tablespoon minced fresh basil

1. Drain and discard gravy from beef; cut roast into 1-inch pieces. Set aside.

2. Heat oil in large skillet over medium-high heat. Add mushrooms; cook and stir 2 to 3 minutes or until lightly browned.

3. Crumble rice in bag. Add rice, water, hoisin sauce and soy sauce to beef mixture. Cover and cook over medium heat 3 to 5 minutes or until mixture is heated through. Stir in green onion and basil; serve immediately.
Makes 4 servings

Country Skillet Supper

1 pound ground beef
1 medium onion, chopped (about ½ cup)
⅛ teaspoon garlic powder *or* 1 clove garlic, minced
1 can (10¾ ounces) CAMPBELL'S Condensed Golden
   Mushroom Soup
1 can (10½ ounces) CAMPBELL'S Condensed Beef Broth
½ teaspoon dried thyme leaves
1 can (14½ ounces) diced tomatoes
1 small zucchini, sliced (about 1 cup)
1½ cups uncooked corkscrew-shaped pasta (rotelle)

1. Cook the beef, onion and garlic powder in a 10-inch skillet over medium-high heat until the beef is well browned, stirring frequently to separate meat. Pour off any fat.

2. Stir the soup, broth, thyme, tomatoes and zucchini into the skillet. Heat to a boil. Stir in the pasta and reduce heat to low. Cook and stir for 15 minutes or until the pasta is tender but still firm.   *Makes 4 servings*

Southwest Skillet

Prep Time: 5 minutes • **Cook Time:** 20 minutes • **Stand Time:** 5 minutes

- **¾ pound ground beef**
- **1 tablespoon chili powder**
- **1 can (10¾ ounces) CAMPBELL'S® Condensed Beefy Mushroom Soup**
- **¼ cup water**
- **1 can (14½ ounces) whole peeled tomatoes, cut up**
- **1 can (about 15 ounces) kidney beans, rinsed and drained**
- **¾ cup uncooked instant rice**
- **½ cup shredded Cheddar cheese (2 ounces)**
- **Crumbled tortilla chips**

1. Cook the beef with chili powder in a 10-inch skillet over medium-high heat until the beef is well browned, stirring frequently to separate meat. Pour off any fat.

2. Stir the soup, water, tomatoes and beans into the skillet. Heat to a boil. Reduce the heat to low. Cover and cook for 10 minutes.

3. Stir the rice into the skillet. Cover the skillet and remove from the heat. Let stand for 5 minutes. Top with the cheese. Serve with the chips.

Makes 4 servings

Ragú®
Chili

2 pounds ground beef
1 large onion, chopped
2 cloves garlic, finely chopped
1 jar (1 pound 10 ounces) RAGÚ® Robusto®! Pasta Sauce
1 can (15 ounces) red kidney beans, rinsed and drained
2 tablespoons chili powder

1. In 12-inch skillet, brown ground beef with onion and garlic over medium-high heat; drain. Stir in remaining ingredients. Simmer uncovered, 20 minutes, stirring occasionally.

2. Serve, if desired, with shredded Cheddar cheese.   *Makes 8 servings*

Beef & Broccoli Pepper Steak

Prep Time: 10 minutes • **Cook Time:** 30 minutes

3 tablespoons butter or margarine, divided
1 pound sirloin or top round steak, cut into thin strips
1 (6.8-ounce) package RICE-A-RONI® Beef Flavor
2 cups broccoli flowerets
½ cup red or green bell pepper strips
1 small onion, thinly sliced

1. In large skillet over medium-high heat, melt 1 tablespoon butter. Add steak; sauté 3 minutes or until just browned. Remove from skillet; set aside.

2. In same skillet over medium heat, sauté rice-vermicelli mix with remaining 2 tablespoons butter until vermicelli is golden brown. Slowly stir in 2½ cups water and Special Seasonings; bring to a boil. Reduce heat to low. Cover; simmer 10 minutes.

3. Stir in steak, broccoli, bell pepper and onion; return to a simmer. Cover; simmer 5 to 10 minutes or until rice is tender.

Makes 4 servings

Veggie Beef
Skillet Soup

¾ pound ground beef
1 tablespoon olive oil
2 cups coarsely chopped cabbage
1 cup chopped green bell pepper
2 cups water
1 can (about 14 ounces) stewed tomatoes
1 cup frozen mixed vegetables
⅓ cup ketchup
1 tablespoon beef bouillon granules
2 teaspoons Worcestershire sauce
2 teaspoons balsamic vinegar
⅛ teaspoon red pepper flakes
¼ cup chopped fresh parsley

1. Brown beef 6 to 8 minutes in large skillet over medium-high heat, stirring to break up meat. Drain fat. Transfer to plate.

2. Heat oil in same skillet. Add cabbage and bell pepper; cook and stir 4 minutes or until cabbage is wilted. Add beef, water, tomatoes, mixed vegetables, ketchup, bouillon, Worcestershire, vinegar and pepper flakes; bring to a boil. Reduce heat; cover and simmer 20 minutes.

3. Remove from heat; let stand 5 minutes. Stir in parsley before serving.

Makes 4 servings

Mexican Casserole
with Tortilla Chips

12 ounces ground beef
1 can (about 14 ounces) stewed tomatoes
1 bag (8 ounces) frozen bell pepper stir-fry mixture, thawed
¾ teaspoon ground cumin
½ teaspoon salt
1½ ounces finely shredded sharp Cheddar cheese
2 ounces tortilla chips, lightly crushed

1. Brown beef 6 to 8 minutes in large nonstick skillet over medium-high heat, stirring to break up meat. Drain fat. Stir in tomatoes, pepper mixture and cumin; bring to a boil. Reduce heat; cover and simmer 20 minutes or until vegetables are tender.

2. Stir in salt. Sprinkle evenly with cheese and chips.

Makes 4 servings

Variation: Sprinkle chips into a casserole. Spread cooked beef mixture evenly over the chips and top with cheese.

Hearty Chili with Black Beans

1 pound ground beef
1 can (about 14 ounces) beef broth
1 onion, minced
1 green bell pepper, seeded and diced
2 teaspoons chili powder
½ teaspoon ground allspice
¼ teaspoon cinnamon
¼ teaspoon paprika
1 can (about 15 ounces) black beans, rinsed and drained
1 can (about 14 ounces) crushed tomatoes
2 teaspoons apple cider vinegar

1. Cook beef, broth, onion and bell pepper 6 to 8 minutes in large skillet over medium-high heat, stirring to break up meat. Drain fat.

2. Stir in chili powder, allspice, cinnamon and paprika. Reduce heat to medium-low; simmer 10 minutes. Stir in black beans, tomatoes and vinegar; bring to a boil.

3. Reduce heat to low; simmer 20 to 25 minutes or until chili is thickened.

Makes 4 servings

Classic Beef Stroganoff

1 cup MINUTE® White Rice, uncooked
1 tablespoon vegetable oil
1 cup onion, chopped
1 pound lean ground beef
2 cups mushrooms, sliced
1 can (14½ ounces) beef broth
1 tablespoon Worcestershire sauce
1 can (10¾ ounces) cream of mushroom soup
½ cup sour cream

Prepare rice according to package directions.

Heat oil in medium skillet over medium-high heat. Add onion; cook and stir 3 minutes. Add beef and brown; drain excess fat.

Add mushrooms, broth, Worcestershire sauce and soup. Bring to a boil and simmer 5 minutes. Stir in sour cream. Serve over rice.

Makes 4 servings

Beef Taco Skillet

Prep Time: 5 minutes • **Cook Time:** 20 minutes

1 pound ground beef
1 can (10¾ ounces) CAMPBELL'S® Condensed Tomato Soup
    (Regular or Healthy Request®)
½ cup salsa
½ cup water
 6 flour tortillas (6-inch), cut into 1-inch pieces
½ cup shredded Cheddar cheese

1. Cook the beef in a 10-inch skillet over medium-high heat until it's well browned, stirring often to separate meat. Pour off any fat.

2. Stir the soup, salsa, water and tortillas in the skillet and heat to a boil. Reduce the heat to low. Cook for 5 minutes. Stir the beef mixture. Top with the cheese.   *Makes 4 servings*

Serving Suggestion: Serve with a mixed green salad with Italian salad dressing and corn on the cob. For dessert, serve with a store-bought flan.

Five-Spice
Beef Skillet

1 boneless beef top sirloin steak (about 1 pound)
2 tablespoons plus 1½ teaspoons cornstarch, divided
2 tablespoons soy sauce
3 tablespoons walnut or vegetable oil, divided
4 carrots, cut into matchstick-size pieces
   (about 2 cups)
3 cups hot cooked rice
1 red bell pepper, cut into 1-inch pieces
1 yellow bell pepper, cut into 1-inch pieces
1 cup chopped onion
¼ to ½ teaspoon red pepper flakes
1½ cups water
1 tablespoon plus 1½ teaspoons packed dark brown sugar
2 teaspoons beef bouillon granules
1 teaspoon Chinese five-spice powder*
½ cup honey-roasted peanuts

Chinese five-spice powder is a blend of cinnamon, cloves, fennel seed, anise and Szechuan peppercorns. It is available in most supermarkets and at Asian grocery stores.

1. Cut steak in half lengthwise, then cut crosswise into thin strips. Place beef in shallow glass baking dish. Combine 2 tablespoons cornstarch and soy sauce in small bowl until well blended. Pour over beef; toss to coat. Marinate 10 minutes.

2. Meanwhile, heat 1 tablespoon oil in large nonstick skillet 1 minute over high heat. Add carrots; cook and stir 3 to 4 minutes or until edges begin to brown. Combine carrots and rice in large bowl; toss well. Cover and keep warm.

3. Reduce heat to medium-high. Add 1 tablespoon oil, bell peppers, onion and pepper flakes; cook and stir 4 minutes or until onion is translucent. Remove mixture to another large bowl. Add remaining 1 tablespoon oil to skillet. Add half of beef; cook and stir 2 minutes or until beef is barely pink in center. Add beef to same large bowl. Repeat with remaining beef.

4. Combine water, sugar, bouillon, five-spice powder and remaining 1½ teaspoons cornstarch in small bowl; stir until smooth. Add bouillon mixture and beef mixture to skillet; bring to a boil. Cook and stir 2 to 3 minutes or until sauce is slightly thickened.

5. Spoon beef mixture over carrot and rice mixture; sprinkle with peanuts.

Makes 4 servings

Herbed Beef & Vegetable Skillet

Prep Time: 10 minutes • **Cook Time:** 20 minutes

2 tablespoons vegetable or canola oil
1 pound boneless beef sirloin or top round steak, ¾-inch thick, cut into thin strips
3 medium carrots, sliced thin diagonally (about 1½ cups)
1 medium onion, chopped (about ½ cup)
2 cloves garlic, minced
½ teaspoon dried thyme leaves, crushed
1 can (10¾ ounces) CAMPBELL'S® Condensed Golden Mushroom Soup
¼ cup water
2 teaspoons Worcestershire sauce
⅛ teaspoon ground black pepper
Hot cooked noodles

1. Heat 1 tablespoon of the oil in a 12-inch skillet over medium-high heat. Add the beef and cook and stir until it's well browned. Remove the beef with a slotted spoon and set it aside.

2. Reduce the heat to medium and add the remaining oil. Add the carrots, onion, garlic and thyme. Cook and stir until the vegetables are tender-crisp.

3. Stir the soup, water, Worcestershire and black pepper into the skillet. Heat to a boil. Return the beef to the skillet and cook until the mixture is hot and bubbling. Serve over the noodles. *Makes 4 servings*

Rapid
Ragú® Chili

Prep Time: 10 minutes • **Cook Time:** 25 minutes

1½ pounds lean ground beef
1 medium onion, chopped
2 tablespoons chili powder
1 can (19 ounces) red kidney beans, rinsed and drained
1 jar (1 pound 10 ounces) RAGÚ® Old World Style® Pasta Sauce
1 cup shredded Cheddar cheese (about 4 ounces)

1. In 12-inch skillet, brown ground beef with onion and chili powder over medium-high heat, stirring occasionally. Stir in beans and Pasta Sauce.

2. Bring to a boil over high heat. Reduce heat to low and simmer covered, stirring occasionally, 20 minutes. Top with cheese. Serve, if desired, over hot cooked rice. *Makes 6 servings*

One-Pan Taco Dinner

Nonstick cooking spray
1 pound lean ground beef
1 packet (1¼ ounces) taco seasoning mix
2 cups water
2 cups MINUTE® White Rice, uncooked
1 cup Cheddar cheese, shredded
2 cups lettuce, shredded
1 large tomato, chopped
Salsa (optional)

Spray large nonstick skillet with nonstick cooking spray. Add beef and brown over medium-high heat; drain excess fat.

Add seasoning mix and water; stir. Bring to a boil. Stir in rice. Sprinkle with cheese; cover. Reduce heat to low; simmer 5 minutes.

Top with lettuce and tomato just before serving. Serve with salsa, if desired. *Makes 4 servings*

Mediterranean Beef Skillet

2½ cups (about 8 ounces) uncooked whole wheat rotini pasta
1 pound ground beef
½ teaspoon dried basil
½ teaspoon black pepper
1 can (about 14 ounces) diced tomatoes with garlic and onion
1 can (8 ounces) tomato sauce
1 bag (about 7 ounces) baby spinach, coarsely chopped
1 can (about 2 ounces) sliced black olives, drained
½ cup crumbled herb-flavored feta cheese

1. Prepare rotini according to package directions; drain. Cover and keep warm.

2. Brown beef 6 to 8 minutes in large skillet over medium-high heat, stirring to break up meat. Drain fat. Stir in basil and pepper.

3. Add tomatoes, tomato sauce, spinach and olives; mix well. Cook over medium heat 10 minutes. Stir in reserved rotini; cook 5 minutes or until heated through. Sprinkle with cheese.   *Makes 4 servings*

Spicy Salsa
Mac & Beef

Prep Time: 5 minutes • **Cook Time:** 20 minutes

1 pound ground beef
1 can (10½ ounces) Campbell's® Condensed Beef Broth
1⅓ cups water
2 cups uncooked medium shell-shaped pasta
1 can (10¾ ounces) Campbell's® Condensed Cheddar Cheese Soup
1 cup chunky salsa

1. Cook the beef in a 10-inch skillet over medium-high heat until the beef is well browned, stirring frequently to separate meat. Pour off any fat.

2. Stir the broth and water into the skillet. Heat to a boil. Add the pasta. Reduce the heat to medium. Cook and stir for 10 minutes or until the pasta is tender but still firm.

3. Stir the soup and salsa into the skillet. Cook and stir until hot and bubbling. *Makes 4 servings*

The publisher would like to thank the companies and organizations listed below for the use of their recipes and photographs in this publication.

Campbell Soup Company

ConAgra Foods, Inc.

Del Monte Foods

The Golden Grain Company®

©2010 Kraft Foods, KRAFT, KRAFT Hexagon Logo, PHILADELPHIA AND PHILADELPHIA Logo are registered trademarks of Kraft Foods Holdings, Inc. All rights reserved.

Lee Kum Kee®

National Pork Board

Ortega®, A Division of B&G Foods, Inc.

Riviana Foods Inc.

Sargento® Foods Inc.

Unilever

VOLUME MEASUREMENTS (dry)

¹/₈ teaspoon = 0.5 mL
¹/₄ teaspoon = 1 mL
¹/₂ teaspoon = 2 mL
³/₄ teaspoon = 4 mL
1 teaspoon = 5 mL
1 tablespoon = 15 mL
2 tablespoons = 30 mL
¹/₄ cup = 60 mL
¹/₃ cup = 75 mL
¹/₂ cup = 125 mL
²/₃ cup = 150 mL
³/₄ cup = 175 mL
1 cup = 250 mL
2 cups = 1 pint = 500 mL
3 cups = 750 mL
4 cups = 1 quart = 1 L

VOLUME MEASUREMENTS (fluid)

1 fluid ounce (2 tablespoons) = 30 mL
4 fluid ounces (¹/₂ cup) = 125 mL
8 fluid ounces (1 cup) = 250 mL
12 fluid ounces (1¹/₂ cups) = 375 mL
16 fluid ounces (2 cups) = 500 mL

WEIGHTS (mass)

¹/₂ ounce = 15 g
1 ounce = 30 g
3 ounces = 90 g
4 ounces = 120 g
8 ounces = 225 g
10 ounces = 285 g
12 ounces = 360 g
16 ounces = 1 pound = 450 g

DIMENSIONS

¹/₁₆ inch = 2 mm
¹/₈ inch = 3 mm
¹/₄ inch = 6 mm
¹/₂ inch = 1.5 cm
³/₄ inch = 2 cm
1 inch = 2.5 cm

OVEN TEMPERATURES

250°F = 120°C
275°F = 140°C
300°F = 150°C
325°F = 160°C
350°F = 180°C
375°F = 190°C
400°F = 200°C
425°F = 220°C
450°F = 230°C

BAKING PAN SIZES

Utensil	Size in Inches/Quarts	Metric Volume	Size in Centimeters
Baking or Cake Pan (square or rectangular)	8×8×2	2 L	20×20×5
	9×9×2	2.5 L	23×23×5
	12×8×2	3 L	30×20×5
	13×9×2	3.5 L	33×23×5
Loaf Pan	8×4×3	1.5 L	20×10×7
	9×5×3	2 L	23×13×7
Round Layer Cake Pan	8×1½	1.2 L	20×4
	9×1½	1.5 L	23×4
Pie Plate	8×1¼	750 mL	20×3
	9×1¼	1 L	23×3
Baking Dish or Casserole	1 quart	1 L	—
	1½ quart	1.5 L	—
	2 quart	2 L	—